USBORNE WORLD WILDLIFE
RAINFOREST WILDLIFE

Antonia Cunningham

Designed by Andrew Dixon and Mary Cartwright

Illustrated by Ian Jackson and David Wright

Series editor: Felicity Brooks

Scientific consultants: Mark Collins and Gill Standring

Additional illustrations by Janos Marffy and Aziz Khan

Contents

Inside the rainforest

Rainforests are some of the oldest and most amazing wild places in the world. They are home to millions of different kinds, or species, of plants and animals. Inside a rainforest, it is always hot, dark and damp. Enormous trees tower about 30m (100ft) above the forest floor, forming a sort of roof which blocks out most of the sunshine. The canopy is so thick that rain can take ten minutes to reach the ground. The main picture shows part of a rainforest in Southeast Asia.

Trees called emergents tower above the canopy.

Canopy

This area between the canopy and the floor is called the understory.

Floor

Macaques

Each part of the forest is home to different animals and plants. Many animals do not travel far. The area that they move around in is called their territory or home range.

Tapir

Porcupine

Habitats and food webs

The type of place where an animal lives is called its habitat. In each habitat there are different types of food. Plants get food from the soil and can make food using sunlight. Animals eat plants or other animals. The way that animals and plants are connected through the food they eat is called a food web. This picture shows part of a food web in a South American rainforest.

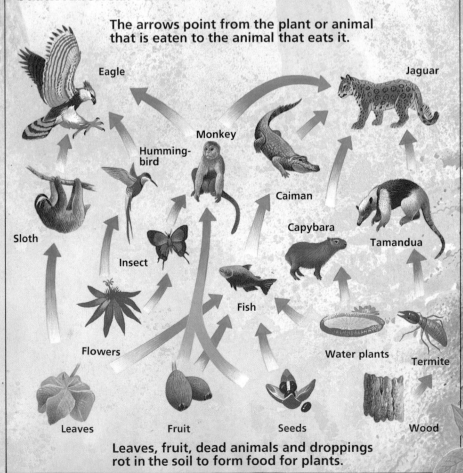

The arrows point from the plant or animal that is eaten to the animal that eats it.

Eagle

Jaguar

Monkey

Humming-bird

Caiman

Sloth

Insect

Capybara

Tamandua

Fish

Flowers

Water plants

Termite

Leaves

Fruit

Seeds

Wood

Leaves, fruit, dead animals and droppings rot in the soil to form food for plants.

Gibbon

Orchids

Tree snake

Rainforest trees never lose all their leaves at once. They are always green. The leaves of different trees never touch.

Dusky leaf monkey

Over half the furry animals in the forest live in the canopy. It is also home to many birds, snakes and frogs.

Big roots called buttress roots grow down from the trunks of the tallest trees. They help to keep the tree upright.

Vines called lianas

Giant squirrel

Pentail tree shrew

Rafflesia

Leopard cat

Many rainforest animals hunt, kill and eat other animals. Animals which hunt are called predators. Animals which are killed are called prey.

Fruit on different trees ripens at different times. Many animals come to eat ripe fruit.

Mouse deer

3

Rainforests of the world

Rainforests grow in an area around the middle of the Earth called the tropics where it is always hot and rainy. In most rainforests, it rains nearly every day and the temperature in the day is usually about 30°C (86°F). These hot, wet forests are called tropical rainforests. The map below shows where the world's tropical rainforests grow.

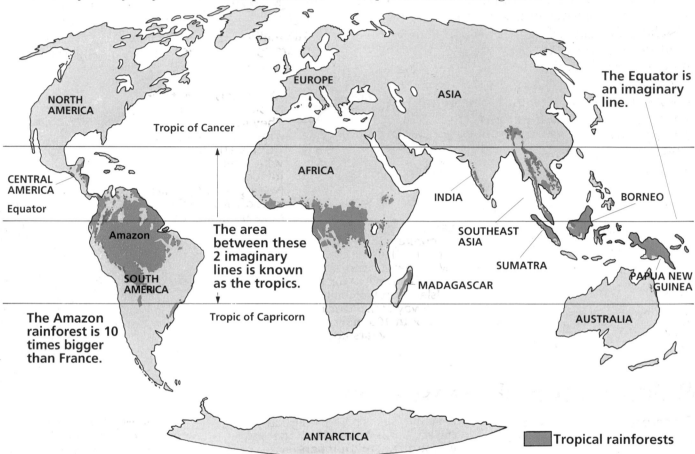

The Equator is an imaginary line.

NORTH AMERICA

EUROPE

ASIA

Tropic of Cancer

CENTRAL AMERICA

AFRICA

INDIA

BORNEO

Equator

Amazon

The area between these 2 imaginary lines is known as the tropics.

SOUTHEAST ASIA

SUMATRA

SOUTH AMERICA

MADAGASCAR

PAPUA NEW GUINEA

The Amazon rainforest is 10 times bigger than France.

Tropic of Capricorn

AUSTRALIA

ANTARCTICA

Tropical rainforests

Forests in danger

Rainforests are in danger because they are being cut down for wood, or to clear land for farming. This means that thousands of plants and animals lose their homes. Many countries have cut down so much rainforest that there is hardly any left. You can find out what people are doing to save rainforests and rainforest animals on pages 30-31.

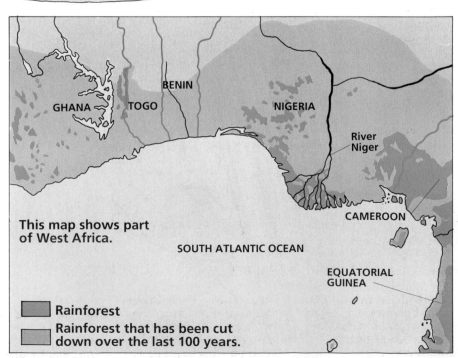

GHANA

BENIN

TOGO

NIGERIA

River Niger

This map shows part of West Africa.

CAMEROON

SOUTH ATLANTIC OCEAN

EQUATORIAL GUINEA

AFRICA

This is the area shown on the big map on the right.

Rainforest

Rainforest that has been cut down over the last 100 years.

Rainforest plants and animals

Every rainforest in the world is different. Many species of animals and plants only live in rainforests in one area. Some scientists think that millions of years ago, all the land on Earth was joined together in one piece. They call this land Pangaea. They think that Pangaea split up over millions of years and that the pieces moved away from each other. This separated the animals and the plants too. Then, over millions of years, the plants and animals changed to suit their habitats. This change is known as adaptation.

200 million years ago

100 million years ago

50 million years ago

Marsupials carry their babies in pouches. They live in South America, Papua New Guinea and Australia, which were all once joined to Antarctica. Nearby islands, which split off from Asia, have no marsupials.

Lemurs are related to monkeys. They live only on the island of Madagascar and the nearby Comoro Islands, which split away from Africa about 100 million years ago.

Ruffed lemur

New Guinea tree kangaroo

Pouch

Rainforests and the weather

Trees help make rain. If they are cut down, it rains less.

1. Trees soak up water through their roots. It goes up into the leaves and branches.

If trees are cut down, rain can cause very bad floods.

2. Water from the leaves goes into the air all the time. When the sun warms them, this happens faster.

4. When the clouds are too heavy, the water falls as rain.

3. The water in the air joins together to form clouds.

Rain trickles through the trees before reaching the ground. Tree roots hold the soil together and soak up water.

When there are no trees, the rain beats down hard, washing away the top layers of soil, which plants need so they can grow.

The soil washes into nearby rivers. Some is washed far away. The soil builds up in rivers and mud banks are formed.

Extra soil in the rivers means there is less room for water. If it rains hard, the rivers overflow, causing bad floods.

Apes and monkeys

Most of the world's monkeys and apes live in rainforests, feeding mainly on fruit and leaves. Monkeys are not apes. They are usually smaller and spend more of their time leaping around in the canopy. They have special thumbs which help them grasp branches easily and most have long tails which help them balance. Monkeys live all over the world, including Asia, Africa and South America. The four types of apes - gibbons, orangutans chimpanzees and gorillas, - have no tails. Gorillas and chimps live in Africa, orangutans and gibbons live in Southeast Asia.

Red uakari

South American monkeys have flat noses and wide nostrils.

Red colobus monkey

Monkeys from Southeast Asia and Africa have narrow noses.

Skeletons

Skeletons help show how animals move. Monkeys have thin hips and long backs, suited to climbing and leaping. Apes have long arms, suited to swinging in trees. Humans have long legs and can walk upright.

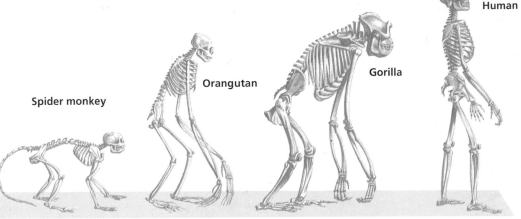

Spider monkey

Orangutan

Gorilla

Human

Gorillas

Gorillas are the largest type of ape. They are very intelligent, peaceful animals. They live in family groups made up of several females and their young, led by a large, adult male. Adult males are called silverbacks because the fur on their backs is silver. Gorillas mainly stay on the ground and spend most mornings and afternoons eating. They rest at midday. At night they sleep in nests made of leaves and broken branches, which are usually raised off the floor of the forest.

Gorillas are vegetarians. They eat leaves and plant stems.

AFRICA

Gorillas live in some parts of Africa. The rarest are mountain gorillas. Only about 600 are left in the wild.

■ Areas where gorillas live

Young adult males leave their family group when they are about 11 to 13 years old. They join or form new families.

Young adult male

Moving through the trees

Brachiating gibbon

Prehensile tails are very strong.

Black-handed spider monkey

Apes and monkeys move through the forest in many ways. Gibbons have long arms and swing between trees, hand over hand, under the branches. This is called brachiating. They can leap distances of up to 15m (50ft). Some South American monkeys have tails called prehensile tails, which they use as extra arms to hang from trees. The ends are very sensitive. Spider monkeys can even use them to pick up nuts.

Silverback

These gorillas are grooming each other.

Female gorillas

Grooming shows that gorillas feel friendly toward each other. Females sometimes groom each other, and often groom their babies and the silverback.

Male gorillas can grow to about 1.7m (5ft 8in) tall. When their arms are spread out they are almost twice as wide as they are tall. In the wild they can live to be about 35 years old.

Young gorillas often play with each other or with the silverback. These gorillas are playing follow the leader.

Females are smaller than males. They grow up to 1.5m (5ft) tall. Baby gorillas start crawling when they are about 9 weeks old and walk after 30 to 40 weeks.

Orangutans

Orangutan means "person of the forest". An adult orangutan is about half as tall as an adult human. Orangutans usually live alone, but babies live with their mothers. Like other apes, females only give birth to one baby at a time. Orangutans rarely come down to the ground. At night, they sleep high up, in nests made out of leaves and broken branches. They mainly eat fruit, leaves and plant shoots. They drink rainwater from holes in trees. They live in Southeast Asia on the islands of Borneo and Sumatra.

Orangutans move through the trees by reaching out and grabbing the next branch or next liana along. They can stretch between branches over 2m (6½ft) apart, which is over twice their own height.

Female orangutan

A baby orangutan clings to its mother's body.

Liana

Adult males have long, dark faces with fatty lumps on each side. In Sumatra they also have beards.

A female orangutan has a baby every 3 to 6 years. A baby rides on its mother's body and sleeps in the same nest until the mother has another baby.

Amazing monkeys

Monkeys can "talk" to each other in many ways. From far away they call to keep in contact with their group and to warn strangers away. Face and body movements can signal feelings. Even skin can show if a monkey is male or female and how important it is in its own group.

Howler monkeys get their name from their very loud calls which can be heard over long distances. Groups of howler monkeys call to each other early each morning.

Black howler monkey

Mandrills have very bright faces and bottoms. Adult males have the most vivid skin. It becomes brighter than usual when they are angry or excited.

Mandrill

Male proboscis monkeys have noses up to 18cm (7in) long. These help them make loud honking noises when they are scared or want to call their group together.

Proboscis monkey

Chimpanzees

There are two types of chimpanzees - common chimps and pygmy chimps. They both live in rainforests in Africa. Chimps mostly eat plants and insects, but some chimps in West Africa have been found which often hunt and eat colobus monkeys.

Termite mound

This chimp is unhappy because he is not getting what he wants.

Monkeys and apes usually show their teeth when they are angry.

Chimps make and use tools. They put nuts or hard-skinned fruit on flat stones and smash them open with rocks.

Chimps poke sticks into termite mounds to catch termites. The termites cover the stick and the chimps eat them.

Before a hunt, chimps drum on tree roots and hoot to call each other. Then, silently, they wander along the forest floor, searching for monkeys in the canopy.

When they see some monkeys, one chimp, who is known as the driver, rushes up a tree and tries to separate one or two monkeys from the main group.

If a monkey is cut off, several chimps, known as blockers, dash into the trees and sit on branches on each side of the monkey's escape route. Other chimps chase it.

The oldest chimp has to guess in advance where the monkey will run. He goes to this place and blocks its escape. The chasers catch the monkey and kill it.

Monkey food

Most monkeys eat leaves and fruit, but some are adapted to eat more unusual things.

Saki

Marmoset

Long-tailed macaque

Sakis place hard seeds in a special gap between their teeth, which makes it easier to crack the seeds open.

Marmosets are the only monkeys that eat gum and sap. They have special teeth which help them gnaw holes in tree trunks to let the gum drip out.

Long-tailed macaques from Southeast Asia live near rivers. They search the mud by the river's edge for crabs, snails and other small animals. They are very good swimmers and often go into the water.

9

The rainforest at night

Rainforests are as busy at night as in the day. When daytime animals go to sleep, many others wake up. These are called nocturnal animals. They call to each other in the darkness. Frogs croak, night monkeys hoot, bushbabies chirp. Nocturnal animals live at all levels in forests all over the world. Deer, okapi, armadillos and agoutis look for food on the ground. Tarsiers, bushbabies and night monkeys live in the canopy and in the understory. Bats flit through the trees. Insects, such as fireflies, signal to each other with bright flashes of light. Even some flowers open up especially at night.

Night monkeys

Bush baby

Armadillo

Night eyes

Eyes need light to work. Light enters a hole in the eye called the pupil. At night there is very little light, so nocturnal animals need big eyes and pupils which let in as much light as possible.

The size of the pupil changes, depending on how much light there is. When there is too much light, the pupils become smaller so the insides of the eyes do not become damaged.

Fishing cat

Tarsiers from Southeast Asia have huge eyes. One eye can weigh as much as their whole brain.

Cat's eye in bright light

Cat's eye in dim light

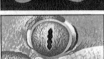
Gecko's eye in bright light

Gecko's eye in dim light

Nocturnal animals have a special layer at the back of their eyes which helps them see at night. It makes their eyes glow in the dark if they are caught in a bright light.

Night life

Scientists do not know exactly why some animals are nocturnal but think that they may prefer the cooler temperature. Night may also be a good time to find food, as fewer animals are feeding. It is also easier to escape from predators in the dark. Some animals do not see well at night, but signal to each other or find food in other ways.

In the mangrove swamps of Southeast Asia, fireflies light up whole trees, flashing on and off together to signal for mates.

Flashing tail

New Guinea tree frog

Throat sac

Frogs croak to call to other frogs. Some have large throat sacs which they fill with air to help them call more loudly.

Pit viper

Pit vipers have little holes in their heads, called pit organs, which can sense the heat other animals give out. This means they can track their prey in the dark.

Pit organ

Bats

There are nearly a thousand different species of bats in the world. Different bats eat fruit, insects, small animals, or a sweet liquid from flowers, called nectar. Many bats live in rainforests. The biggest are Malay fruit bats (also called flying foxes), which live in Southeast Asia. During the day, thousands of fruit bats hang upside-down by their claws in the tops of trees or in caves. At night they may fly as far as 70km (over 40 miles) to find food.

1st finger

2nd finger

Thumb

3rd finger

4th finger

Malay fruit bat

When its wings are open, a Malay fruit bat is over 1.3m (4ft 2in) wide - about as wide as you are, when you hold your arms out.

Head looks like a fox's head.

Bat wings have fingers, thumbs and claws. The claws can grip firmly when the bat is hanging upside-down.

Kitti's hog-nosed bat

Claws are curved and sharp.

Kitti's hog-nosed bats are the world's smallest bats. They weigh 1.5g (0.05oz) and are only 15cm (6in) wide with their wings open. You can hold one in the palm of your hand.

Finding food

Bats find food in different ways. Some, such as fruit bats, can see and smell their food. Fringe-lipped bats find frogs to eat by listening for the frogs' mating calls. Other bats track insects by using a method called echo-location, which is shown in these pictures.

Bats let out high-pitched squeaks as they fly. The sounds bounce off objects, and back to the bats as echoes.

Bats know from the echoes if the object is an insect. They track an insect by following the changing direction of the echoes.

They grab their prey in their mouths and eat it as they fly. Some insects can hear bat squeaks and avoid being caught.

Gliders

Some animals can glide from tree to tree instead of leaping. This is a good way to travel long distances and escape most predators. However, gliders are still easy targets for hungry birds. To lessen the danger, many of them are patterned to blend in with their surroundings. Most of them only come out at night when it is harder for predators to spot them.

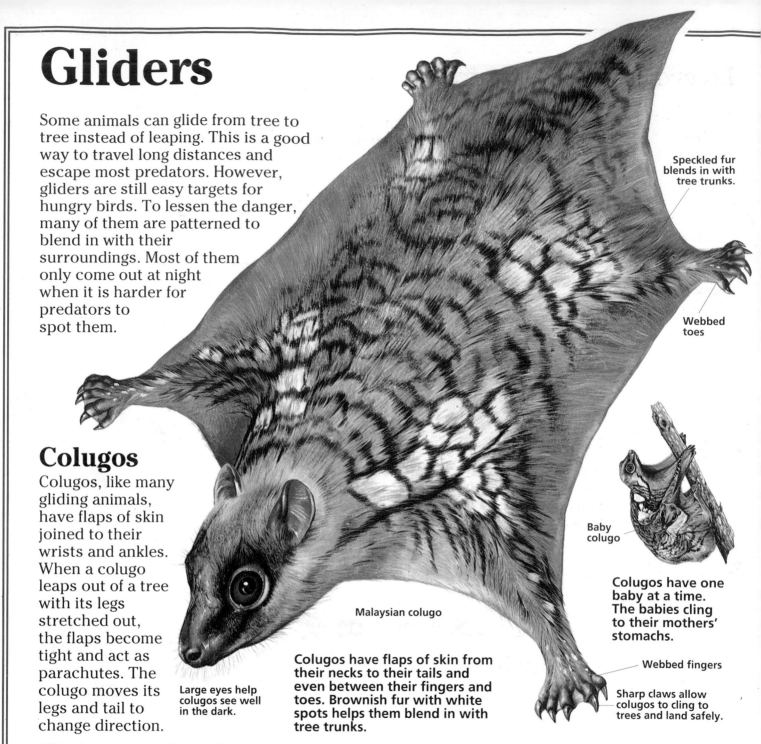

Speckled fur blends in with tree trunks.

Webbed toes

Colugos

Colugos, like many gliding animals, have flaps of skin joined to their wrists and ankles. When a colugo leaps out of a tree with its legs stretched out, the flaps become tight and act as parachutes. The colugo moves its legs and tail to change direction.

Large eyes help colugos see well in the dark.

Malaysian colugo

Colugos have flaps of skin from their necks to their tails and even between their fingers and toes. Brownish fur with white spots helps them blend in with tree trunks.

Baby colugo

Colugos have one baby at a time. The babies cling to their mothers' stomachs.

Webbed fingers

Sharp claws allow colugos to cling to trees and land safely.

Flying squirrels

Flying squirrels sleep in the day in tree holes. In Indonesia and Malaysia some make nests in coconut shells. At dusk, they climb into the tree tops to feed on leaves, plant shoots and nuts.

Flying squirrels launch themselves into the air, with their front and back legs stretched out.

They can glide as far as 100m (328ft) between trees. They often travel long distances to find food.

When they land, they turn around to face downward, ready to rush to safety in a tree hole if necessary.

Lizards, snakes and frogs

When a lizard is feeding or resting, its flaps are folded away against its body.

Flying lizards are some of the most common gliders in Southeast Asian rainforests. They are about 15cm (6in) long and have flying flaps joined to their ribs. To fly, they pull their ribs out, making a stiff flap on each side. Then they leap into the air. They can glide up to 15m (50ft) between trees and can change position and roll over while in the air.

Flying lizard

Ribs

Three species of tree snakes can glide. They do not have flying flaps. Instead, they raise their rib-cages upward and outward. This flattens out their bodies which then act like parachutes. With S-shaped movements from side to side, a snake can glide as far as 50m (165ft).

Ornate flying snake

Flying snake's ribs when resting

Flying snake's ribs when flying

Flying fish

Freshwater hatchet fish in the Amazon River can glide in the air up to 10m (33ft). Scientist think they may even really fly, flapping their fins.

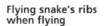

South American gliding tree frog

Webs

Several tree frogs glide. They have long, widely-spaced toes with webs between them. These help them glide in the way that flying flaps do. Gliding frogs use their legs to steer to the left or right as they glide. They can cover gaps up to 12m (40ft) wide.

Plants

Half of all plant species grow in rainforests. Many different kinds of plants can grow in a very small area. In Costa Rica, for example, scientists discovered 233 species in an area about a tenth of the size of a soccer field.

Orchids

There are over 35,000 species of orchids in the world. More than three-quarters of them grow in rainforests.

Finding food and water

Rainforest plants grow down near the forest floor, high in the trees, and even on other plants. They get some food from the soil but they also make their own food from sunlight which they take in through their leaves. Different plants can survive on different amounts of light. Plants that need lots of light grow high up in the trees and their roots take in water from the air. Plants that survive on less light live nearer the ground.

Bromeliads mostly grow in the canopy. They fill with rainwater and many small animals live in the water, trapped between their leaves. Some bromeliads can hold up to 54 litres (12 gallons) of water.

Bromeliad

Leaves up in the canopy take in a great deal of sunlight.

Many orchids grow in the canopy.

Moss

Orchid

Roots

Liana

Woody vines called lianas climb into the tree tops to reach the sun. They often stretch between trees and hang in thick loops.

Many leaves have pointed ends called drip tips. When it rains, the rain runs off the drip tip. This helps the leaf dry quickly and stops moss from growing on it and blocking out the light.

Drip tip

Pitcher plants

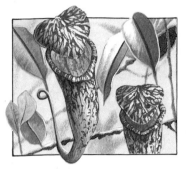 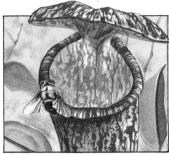  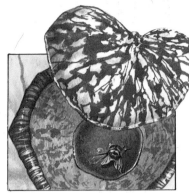

Pitcher plants catch insects. They have jug-shaped leaves which are about half full of a special liquid.

Insects are attracted by the way the plant smells and looks. They land on the rim of the jug, looking for food.

The rim of the jug is waxy and the insects slip and fall into the liquid. They cannot climb up the sides to get out again.

The liquid makes the insects dissolve (like salt in hot water). The plant takes in the dissolved insects as food.

Attracting animals

Plants often need animals, such as insects, birds and bats to help them spread seeds. The animals help do this when they fly from flower to flower, feeding on nectar, a sweet liquid food. When an animal puts its head inside a flower to sip the nectar, it becomes covered in a golden dust called pollen. When it feeds on another flower, the pollen rubs off. If the flowers belong to the same species, the pollen will make the second plant grow seeds. Animals are usually only attracted to certain flowers. This makes them more likely to carry pollen between flowers of the same species.

Scarlet honey-eater

Most birds cannot smell, but can see very well. Flowers which mainly attract birds are very bright, often orange or red. They do not often have a strong smell.

Banana Flower

Some bats can smell and see well. Flowers which attract them smell damp and only open at night. The bats can see them in the dark because most are pale.

Flying fox

Orchid

Carpenter bee

Some flowers have a special smell which attracts only one type of insect. One species of orchid attracts only male carpenter bees because they smell like female carpenter bees.

Jungle giants

The hot, wet weather in rainforests helps many plants grow to huge sizes.

Rafflesia plants have the world's biggest flowers. They are 1m (3ft) across and weigh 6kg (13lbs). Rafflesias smell of rotting meat. This attracts insects that feed on the bodies of dead animals.

Rafflesia flower

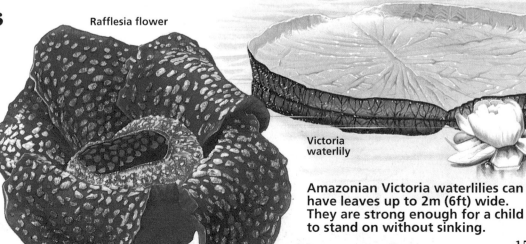

Victoria waterlily

Amazonian Victoria waterlilies can have leaves up to 2m (6ft) wide. They are strong enough for a child to stand on without sinking.

Wild cats

Over three-quarters of all types of wild cats live in forests. Most of these live in rainforests. Cats vary in size but they are all meat eaters, have excellent eyesight, can run very fast and are good tree climbers. Most of them are also nocturnal. Big cats can roar but small cats can only purr and meow. Most cats usually live and hunt alone. They mark out their territory, or home range, by leaving smells or claw marks on trees and rocks which warn other cats to stay away. The cats on these pages all live in rainforests, but many of them can also live in other types of forest, or on open grassland.

Jaguars

Jaguars are the only big cats that live in Central and South America. They are very good swimmers and like living in thick forest, near water. They mainly eat animals such as peccaries, capybaras and fish. They sometimes even catch and eat crocodiles.

Every jaguar has a different pattern of whiskers and coat markings in the same way as every human has a different set of finger prints.

At birth, jaguars are less than 40cm (16in) long. They are born with their eyes shut. These open up after about 13 days.

Some jaguars are born with black fur. They are not a different species of jaguar.

In the dark, jaguars and other big cats can see about 6 times better than humans. They have very strong jaws and teeth which can bite through bones very easily.

Cubs stay with their mothers for about 2 years. They can have babies themselves when they are about 3 years old.

Coat markings

Wild cats usually have yellow or brownish fur with spotted or striped markings. At night, or in the patchy daylight of the forest, this helps them blend in with the light and shade of their surroundings. This makes it easier for them to hide when they are hunting.

Because most animals can only see in black and white, this is what a clouded leopard in a tree would look like to them. Notice how the its patterned markings help break up the outline of its body against its background.

Clouded leopard

Tigers

Tigers are the largest cats. They are very strong and can catch big animals and drag them away. Sometimes they attack baby elephants. They hunt alone and often travel 10 to 20km (6 to 12 miles) a night to find food. Only about one hunt in 20 is successful. If they cannot find big animals, they eat small ones, such as ants or frogs. They each eat about six tonnes (6½ tons) of meat a year, about the same amount of meat as in over 58,000 hamburgers.

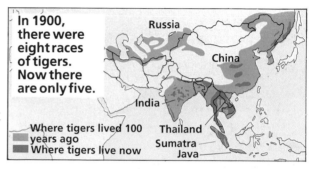

In 1900, there were eight races of tigers. Now there are only five.

Russia
China
India
Thailand
Sumatra
Java

Where tigers lived 100 years ago
Where tigers live now

When a tiger sees an animal, it hides a short distance away, waiting to attack.

It moves forward slowly, and when it gets near enough it rushes forward.

It pounces on the animal from the side or from the back and digs its claws in.

The animal falls down and the tiger bites it in the neck or throat to kill it.

Sometimes, when a tiger kills a large animal, other tigers come and eat it too.

Cat sizes

Here you can see how long some cats are when you compare them with each other.

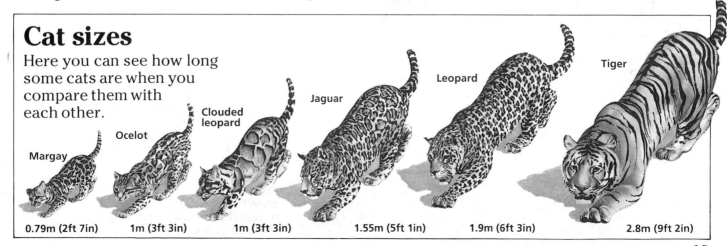

Margay
Ocelot
Clouded leopard
Jaguar
Leopard
Tiger

0.79m (2ft 7in)   1m (3ft 3in)   1m (3ft 3in)   1.55m (5ft 1in)   1.9m (6ft 3in)   2.8m (9ft 2in)

Rivers and streams

Rivers and streams run through every rainforest in the world. The River Amazon in South America is 6,400km (4,000 miles) long. It is mostly 2 to 5km (1 to 3 miles) wide, but near the sea, it can be as much as 320km (200 miles) wide. It is home to thousands of species of plants and animals, some of which you can see here. Deep in the forest, the main river splits up into over a thousand smaller rivers and streams.

In the rainy season the Amazon overflows and floods the nearby forest for up to 6 months.

Forest that becomes flooded

Unflooded forest

Level of river in rainy season

Normal level of river

Capybaras are the world's largest rodents. Like other rodents, such as guinea pigs and rats, they have large front teeth for gnawing.

Capybaras

Otter cubs

Giant otters live in groups of up to 15. They build dens in the river bank, and mark their home range with droppings. When swimming, they hum and chuckle to each other. They scream when scared.

Dolphins

Otters hold fish in their paws when they eat them.

Caimans, a type of crocodile, are now rare because people hunt them for their skins and steal their eggs.

Caimans

Under the water

There are 2,000 to 3,000 species of fish in the Amazon - ten times as many as in Europe. Some eat small animals and other fish. Others eat fruit and seeds that fall into the water.

Most piranhas eat seeds and nuts, but some eat meat. These swim in large groups and can eat an animal in a few minutes.

Piranhas

Tambaqui fish can eat up to 1kg (2.2lbs) of seeds each time they feed.

Teeth and jaws crush seeds

Tambaqui fish

Arapaima

Arapaimas are the biggest freshwater fish in the world. They grow to at least 3m (9 ft 10in) long and weigh up to 200kg (440lbs).

Mangrove swamps

Forests change near the ocean. The river is salty and its level falls and rises with the ocean tides. The ground is always muddy. Tree roots cannot take in oxygen from mud, so they grow above the ground and take oxygen from the air. These areas near the ocean are called mangrove swamps. Here are some of the animals that live there.

Water at low tide

Mangrove tree roots

Fiddler crab

Male fiddler crabs have a big claw which they wave at females.

Mudskippers are fish which can live in and out of water. They twitch their bodies to jump around on tree roots.

Mudskipper

Anableps

Anableps have eyes which are split in two so they can see above and below the water at the same time.

Blue and yellow macaws

Red uakari monkeys

There are 2 types of Amazon River dolphins. They are nearly blind and find their way by echo-location, like bats, sending out rapid clicks through the water. They may also "talk" to each other with clicks.

Red ibises

Red ibises are wading birds. They poke their beaks into the mud to search for food.

Manatees are the largest animals in the river. They grow up to 2.5m (8ft 2in) long. Scientists think they are distant relatives of elephants.

Nostrils

Amazon kingfisher

Electric eel

Manatee

Electric eels kill fish and other animals with shocks of up to 650 volts, enough to stun a horse.

Manatees eat about 20kg (44lbs) of plants a day. They close their nostrils under water and can stay there for an hour at a time. They taste and smell things with their tongues.

Reptiles and amphibians

Hundreds of different species of reptiles and amphibians live in rainforests. They live on the ground, in the trees, in and near water and even inside plants. Reptiles are scaly animals such as crocodiles, snakes and lizards which mainly live on land. Amphibians, such as frogs and toads, can live both in and out of water. You can see some of these animals here.

Snakes

Snakes live in trees and on the ground. Some use poison to kill their prey. The poison comes through their sharp teeth, called fangs. All snakes can open their mouths very wide to eat prey. If the prey is big their stomachs stretch so that it fits. Most snakes only need to eat about nine times a year.

Some snakes push the tube that they breathe through to the front of their mouths when they eat. This helps them breathe.

Breathing tube

Poison sac

Muscle stretches so jaw bones can separate.

Fangs

Upper jaw

Lower jaw

The fer de lance is the most poisonous snake in South America.

A snake's upper and lower jaw can come apart so they can stretch their mouths to swallow big prey.

Emerald tree boas have prehensile tails. They use them to hang from branches and catch passing birds.

Emerald tree boa

Anaconda

Caiman

Gaboon viper

Snakes flick their tongues in and out to pick up smells in the air. They can recognize the smells of different animals and follow smells to find food or a mate.

An anaconda can open its mouth incredibly wide to eat big prey.

Anacondas live near rivers. They are among the world's biggest snakes. They can grow up to 12m (39ft) long. Like some other big snakes, they kill by wrapping themselves tightly around their prey to stop it from breathing. They even kill and eat caimans.

Laying eggs

Most frogs and toads lay eggs in or near water and leave them. The eggs hatch into tadpoles which slowly change into tiny frogs or toads. In some cases, however, the adults look after their eggs and young.

Vocal sac

Male Darwin frogs keep their eggs in their vocal sacs. The eggs hatch and the frogs hop out when they have grown.

Hole

Male Surinam toads put their eggs in holes on the female's back where they hatch straight into toads.

Arrow-poison frogs carry their tadpoles from where they hatch.

They put each tadpole into a water-filled plant in the canopy.

The female feeds them each week with eggs that will not grow.

The tadpoles slowly grow into frogs in these tiny ponds.

Avoiding danger

Reptiles and amphibians have many ways of avoiding being eaten.

Arrow-poison frog

Arrow-poison frogs have different bright patterns to warn predators that they are very poisonous.

Skink

Some lizards, such as skinks, make their tails fall off if they are attacked. This confuses the predator and the lizard escapes.

Turtles have hard shells to protect them. Matamata turtles have bumpy shells which look like dead leaves.

Matamata turtle

Chameleon

Chameleons take on the colour of their surroundings so they cannot be seen easily.

Crocodiles

Crocodiles and alligators are the nearest living relatives to dinosaurs. They have hardly changed in 65 million years. They bask in the sun by rivers in the day and hunt in the water in the evening. They eat fish and insects, but also much bigger animals.

Nests are 2-3m (6-10ft) high.

See-through eyelids cover a crocodile's eyes under water. A flap of skin covers the back of its throat to stop it from swallowing water.

A crocodile uses its webbed feet for paddling slowly. It moves its strong tail from side to side when it swims fast.

A crocodile's eyes and nostrils are almost on top of its head so it can see and breathe when it is halfway under the water.

Some crocodiles make big nests to keep their eggs warm. Others bury their eggs in the ground. The young dig their way out when they hatch.

Insects and spiders

At least two-thirds of all living species on Earth are spiders and insects. Some of the most amazing and beautiful ones live in rainforests. Insects are always in danger of being eaten by larger animals, so many of them have ways of blending in with their surroundings which makes it more difficult for predators to spot them.

Some moths look like parts of trees.

This mantis looks like the flower it lives in.

This katydid looks like a leaf.

Beetles and butterflies

Most butterflies and beetles live in the tropics. There are so many that some do not have everyday names, only a scientific one. (These names are written in *italics*.) Butterflies live in the canopy, near flowers and water. Beetles live everywhere in the forest. Over 500 species of beetles can be found in one tree.

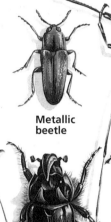

Metallic beetle

Harlequin longhorn beetle

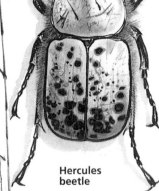

Hercules beetle

Giant weevil   **Giraffe weevil**   **Palm weevil**

Longhorn beetle

Rhinoceros beetle

Violin beetle

Agrias aedon

Papilio karna

Agrias claudina   *Perisama vaninka*   *Idea jasonia*

Callicore mengeli   *Callicore cyllene*   *Callicore cajetani*   *Perisama eminens*

Agrias claudina   *Callithea optima*   *Callithea davisi*

Butterfly disguises

Many butterflies have very vivid patterns to warn predators that they taste unpleasant. Some harmless butterflies copy the appearance of bad tasting ones to trick predators into leaving them alone. Sometimes females of the same species do not look alike because in different places they copy the warning patterns of different types of poisonous butterflies.

Male mocker swallowtail butterfly from Africa

Female mocker swallowtail butterflies

24

Hunting spiders

Spiders are predators. Thousands of species live in rainforests. They hunt their food in different ways. Many of them catch insects and even small birds or reptiles in webs made out of spider silk. They kill their prey by biting it. Some spiders bite poison into their prey to stop it from struggling. Others wrap it up in silk. The silk comes from the spiders' bodies. It dries hard as soon as it reaches the air. Some spiders can make as much as 300m (nearly 1,000ft) of silk a day.

Wandering spider

Hairy body

Fangs

Tree frog

Spiders cannot eat solid food so they bite special juices into their prey to make its insides become liquid.

Large wandering spiders are about 8cm (3in) long. They hunt at night, catching insects and other small animals, such as tree frogs.

Nephila spiders make very strong silk which can even trap small animals. Some local fishermen use their silk to make fishing nets.

Gladiator spiders weave sticky silk nets which they drop onto their prey as it passes below them.

Argiope spiders spin patterned webs. Insects mistake the patterns for flowers and fly into the webs.

Crab spider

Crab spiders match the flowers they live in. They wait for insects to come to feed and then kill them.

Trapdoor tricks

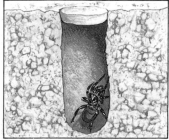

A trapdoor spider lives in a silk-lined burrow with a trapdoor entrance.

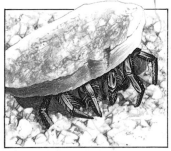

It lies in wait just under the door, sometimes with its legs sticking out.

It feels the ground move when an insect passes and rushes out to attack it.

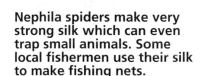

It kills the insect and drags it in. It sucks out the insect's insides.

The rainforest floor

Animals that live on the rainforest floor are not often seen by people. Some only come out at night. Others are very small, or patterned so that they match their habitat and are difficult to see. Most of them feed on plants, roots, fallen fruit, insects or dead wood and leaves.

Forest elephants from India and Southeast Asia have small ears and short tusks. They use their trunks to reach for leaves on trees. Sometimes, if they cannot reach high enough, they push over small trees.

Asian elephant

Sumatran rhinoceros

Okapi

Okapis in Africa are related to giraffes. Their striped markings make them hard to see in the forest.

Agouti

Peccary

Forest rhinos live in Southeast Asia. They eat leaves, can run fast and use their horns to fight.

Porcupine

Malaysian porcupines have sharp spines. When they attack, they raise their spines, rattle their spiny tails and charge backward at their enemy.

Peccaries and agoutis sniff around on the ground looking for plant roots, nuts and seeds. They are the only animals, apart from parrots, that can crack open the hard shells of Brazil nuts.

Pangolin

Royal antelope

Goliath frog

Royal antelopes in Africa are 30cm (1ft) tall and weigh 2.5kg (5.5lbs). This is less than African Goliath frogs which weigh up to 3.1kg (6.8lbs).

Pangolins are covered in hard scales which predators cannot bite through. They use their long tongues to lick up ants and termites. Some species live mainly on the ground. Others live in trees.

Birds on the ground

Many birds spend a great deal of time on the ground. They may fly up into the trees to escape from predators.

Peacocks live in Southeast Asia. The males display their beautiful feathers to show off to females.

These are jungle fowl. Domestic chickens are descended from them.

Great argus pheasants have tail feathers which are 1 to 1.5m (3 to 5ft) long.

Megapode birds

Megapode birds have big feet, which they use to push soil and leaves together to make big mounds. They bury their eggs inside these mounds.

The mounds are about 1.5m (5ft) high. The eggs are kept warm by the sun and by heat from the dead leaves which start to rot in the soil.

The male bird tests the temperature of the mound with his beak. If it is too hot or too cold, he takes away or adds some soil.

The chicks dig their way out and run off after they hatch. They fly within a few hours. The parents do not look after them at all.

Ants and termites

Many insects, such as ants and termites, live on the forest floor in large groups called colonies. Some termites live in rotting wood and others build mounds out of soil, their own droppings and saliva.

The queen is huge. She mates with the king. She is the only one that can lay eggs. She lays thousands of eggs every day.

Queen

King

Soldier termites defend the colony. They have bigger heads and jaws than workers.

Soldier

Workers

Termites called workers build the mound, find food and look after the queen.

Some workers grow food for the colony. They build their droppings into structures called combs. Fungus grows on the combs. Then the termites eat both the fungus and the combs.

Inside a termite mound

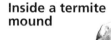

Strong, hard walls made out of droppings, saliva and soil

Fungus chamber

Comb

Royal chamber for king and queen

27

Rainforest people

People have been living in groups, called tribes, in rainforests for about 40,000 years. The forest provides them with everything they need to survive. They hunt animals, gather plants and fruit, and some tribes grow crops. They build their homes out of parts of trees and plants and know how to use hundreds of different plants as medicines.

The Penan tribe live in Sarawak in Malaysia.

The Kayapo Indians are a tribe that live in Brazil.

Yanomami Indians

Area where the Yanomami live

The Yanomami Indians live in Brazil in small villages. In each village all the people live in one big, round house called a yano. Yanos are always built close to rivers and are surrounded by gardens where the villagers grow up to 60 different crops. Half the gardens are planted with banana and plantain trees. The rest are planted with other crops, such as corn, cassava (a root vegetable), sweet potatoes, and fruit, such as papaya. Only about 20 crops are used for food, the rest are used for medicines, religious ceremonies, or for making things.

Women look after the crops and gather food from the forest.

Each family has a fire which they keep burning day and night.

Yano

The central space is used for dancing and ceremonies.

The Yanomami keep pets such as monkeys and macaws.

A yano is made from trees. The roof is made of palm leaves.

Families live under the roofed part of the yano. They sleep in hammocks.

Bananas and plantains are often eaten. They are roasted, boiled or made into soup.

Women dry, grate and sieve cassava (also called manioc) to make a kind of bread.

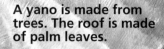

28

Hunting

Yanomami men go hunting almost every day. Boys start to go hunting when they are about five years old. Each morning the hunters go into the forest alone or in groups of two or three. They hunt with large blowpipes, bows and poison-tipped arrows. It takes a long time for a hunter to learn how to use weapons well. Good hunters are highly respected in the tribe.

The Yanomamis hunt with very big weapons.

Shamans

The Yanomami Indians believe that everything has a spirit and that these spirits can affect their everyday lives. Spirits must be respected otherwise they will cause illness and other troubles which can only be cured by healers, called shamans. When someone is ill, a shaman dances and sings to call good spirits down from the sky to help find out which bad spirit is causing the illness. The good spirits help send the bad spirits away so the ill person gets well.

Before a healing ceremony, a shaman paints his body and breathes in a special powder which makes him see visions.

A shaman dances and chants to a bad spirit calling it out of an ill person's body. This ceremony can last many hours.

A shaman dancing

Feasts and stories

Members of a village often invite friends and family from other places to a feast. It takes several days to get the feast ready. Before the feast, the Yanomami paint patterns on their bodies. The feast may last many days. It is a Yanomami custom to be very generous. Both villages give each other presents and there is a lot of singing, dancing and story telling. Here is a story about how some birds got red feathers.

One day two girls came to the home of Opossum and his mother, the Mushroom Woman. He offered them food but they said it all smelled bad.

He sent them to a friend's home to get some tobacco. The friend, a man called Honey, was so handsome that the girls forgot about Opossum.

Opossum became jealous and that night he shot Honey with a magic dart and killed him. Soon everyone knew about this.

Opossum was so scared he grew feathers and flew away, but the birds, led by Toucan, found and killed him and painted themselves with his blood.

The blood never came off, which is why some birds now have red markings. Toucan gave each bird a rock to live in and they became the first forest spirits.

Rainforests in danger

Rainforest people, animals and plants are dying out because the forests are being cut down to make room to grow crops, to farm cattle, to search for coal and precious metals in the ground, or to sell the wood from the trees. If this continues, rainforests will disappear forever and many things, such as the weather, will change. Many people, plants and animals have already died out and many others are in danger.

The animals shown here are all endangered species. This means that there are very few of them left in the wild and they could easily die out.

Hyacinth macaw

A third of all parrots are endangered, including hyacinth macaws, the largest parrots in the world.

Golden lion tamarin

Golden lion tamarins are among the most endangered species of monkeys in the world.

Humboldt's woolly monkeys have been hunted almost to extinction.

Humboldt's woolly monkey

Homerus swallowtail butterfly

Homerus swallowtail butterflies are among the world's rarest butterflies.

Plants and medicines

Rainforests provide many things which we use. For example, many of our foods come from rainforests. Over a quarter of all medicines are made out of rainforest plants and there are still thousands of plants that scientists and doctors do not know about. It would be better to learn how to use things from the rainforests without damaging them, than to cut them all down so that there are none left in the future.

Bananas

Rice

Coffee

Oranges

Pineapple

Lemons

Avocados

Many foods come from plants that first grew in rainforests.

A medicine made out of rosy periwinkles from Madagascar is used to treat a type of cancer called leukaemia.

Rosy periwinkle

Saving the rainforest

There are some things being done to save rainforests. Areas of land called national parks, or reserves, have been set aside where people, animals, and plants can live safely. Projects are being set up to save some species of animals and plants which are very rare. Some laws have been passed to protect rainforests and rare animals.

Mountain gorillas live in national parks on the borders of Rwanda, Zaire and Uganda in Africa. By 1978 they were almost extinct, and some conservation groups and the government of Rwanda, set up the Mountain Gorilla Project to try to save them. They organized guards to protect the gorillas from hunters, taught local people how important the gorillas were and set up tourist trips to help make money for the park. The gorillas and their habitat are now safe.

Local people work in the Rwandan national park. It is now important to Rwanda because it makes money.

Since 1960, miners and road builders have been working in the Brazilian rainforest. They have cut down a lot of forest and many Yanomami Indians have lost their homes. Some have also caught diseases, such as mumps, from the workers, and died. Survival International (see right) set up a campaign to try to save the Yanomami. In 1991, the president of Brazil finally agreed to turn Yanomami lands into a national park.

In 1983, people from 13 Yanomami villages died from disease when a road was built through their lands.

Joining a group

There are many international groups who work to save the rainforests and the people and animals that live there. You can become a member and find out what you can do to help.

Survival International is a world-wide organization which helps tribal people. It believes they should decide their own future and helps them to save their homes and way of life.

For more information write to:

**Survival International,
310 Edgware Road,
London W2 1DY,
UK**

Survival
for tribal peoples

This is the symbol of Survival International.

The World Wide Fund for Nature (WWF)* teaches people about looking after nature and raises money to protect species and habitats all around the world.

For more information write to:

**Information Division,
WWF International,
Avenue du Mont-Blanc,
CH-1196 Gland,
Switzerland**

The giant panda is the symbol of the WWF.

The International Council for Bird Preservation (ICBP) works to save endangered birds.

For more information write to:

**ICBP,
32 Cambridge Road,
Girton,
Cambridge,
CB3 0PJ,
UK**

This is the symbol of the ICBP.

Index